Country Divas

Cherry Lane Music Company
Director of Publications/Project Editor: Mark Phillips

ISBN 1-57560-750-6

Visit our website at www.cherrylane.com 

CONTENTS

Back in Baby's Arms
Words and Music by
Bob Montgomery
Happily with a bounce (in 2)
A♭6
E♭(add9)
1
2
E♭7
A♭
Fm
E♭
D♭
Cm
I'm back in baby's arms.
How I missed those lovin' arms.
I'm back where I be-

B♭m
A♭
E♭7
To Coda
long. back in ba - by's
A♭6
arms. Don't
E♭7
know why we quar - relled,
A♭
we nev - er did be - fore.

Fm
Since we found out
Cm
how it hurts
Db
I bet we nev - er
Eb
quar - rel
Ab
an - y - more.
D.S. al Coda
CODA
Ab6
arms.
Eb(add9)

A6
E(add9)
A6
E7
Thought I did - n't need his
love till he took it a - way.
A
F♯m
C♯m
Now I'm back where I be -

D
E
long and in my ba - by's arms I'm gon - na
A6
stay.
I'm
E7
back in ba - by's arms.
How I
A
missed those lov - in' arms.

F#m
E
D
C#m
I'm back where I be - long back in ba - by's arms.
Bm
A
E7
A6
E(add9)
Back in ba - by's arms.
A6
Repeat and Fade

Backseat of a Greyhound Bus

Words and Music by
Aimee Mayo, Hillary Lindsey,
Chris Lindsey and Troy Verges

E
all they do is talk.
on the in - ter - state.
Bm7
No wed - ding ring, chipped fin - ger - nail pol - ish, she al - ways wished that she could
Some - where be - tween Jack - son and Mem - phis she fin - 'lly found what
A
go to col - lege, but some dreams fade, they just slip a -
she had been miss - in', she cried out - loud while the red
E
E/G♯
way. She start - ed to show
lights flashed. Sweet ba - by girl,

A
E/B
a few months a - go and she had to go, that's
well she looked in - to the face of a new, the
B
E
how she wound up
face of a brand new world
on the back - seat of a Grey -
E/G♯
- hound bus,
head on down with the win - dows up.
heart so full that it could bust.
A
D
Star - in' at the rest of her life.

A/C#
E
She nev - er thought this would be the place where
E/G#
A
she would find her sav - in' grace, but she fell in love,
C#m
D
To Coda
she fell in love on the back seat of a
1
A/C#
E
Grey - hound bus.
2
A/C#
Grey - hound bus.

E
B
Ah,
ah,
C#m
4fr
A
ah,
ah,
ah.
E/G#
Asus2
Sweet ba - by girl, she found
E/B
B
D.S. al Coda
a brand new world on the

CODA
A/C♯
E
Grey - hound bus.
Bm7
A
E
She wore a dress with cher -
- ries on it,
Bm7
go - in' some - where where she'd be want - ed,

Asus2
E
hey,
yeah.
Na na na na na na na na na na na
Bm7
A
na na,
oh,
Repeat and Fade
Optional Ending
E
E
yeah.

Can't Fight the Moonlight

Words and Music by
Diane Warren

A
Em7
un - til, 'til the sun goes down. Un - der - neath the star -
too long 'til you're in my arms. Un - der - neath the star -
D
Em7
D/F♯
light, star - light, there's a mag - i - cal feel - ing so right.
light, star - light, we'll be lost in a rhy - thm so right.
G
G5
N.C.
Chorus:
Cm
It will take you in to - night.
Feel it steal your heart to - night.
You can try to re - sist, try to hide
Fm7
B♭
A♭
G
from my kiss, but you know, but you know that you can't fight the moon - light. Deep

Cm
Fm7
in the dark, you'll sur - ren - der your heart. Don't you know,
B♭
A♭
G
Fm7
don't you know that you can't fight the moon - light, no, you can't fight
1.
G7
G/B
it. It's gon - na get to your heart.
2.
G7
it.
Fm7
G7
N.C.
No mat - ter what you do the night is gon - na get to you.

Bridge:
Bm7
Em7
A
Can't fight it. Don't try it, you're nev-
er gon-na win, cuz,
Fm7
un-der-neath the star-
E♭
Fm7
E♭/G
light, star-light, there's a mag-i-cal feel-ing so right.
A♭
A♭5
It will steal your heart to-night. You can try

Chorus:
C♯m
F♯m7
B
to re - sist, try to hide from my kiss, but you know, but you know that you
A
G♯
C♯m
F♯m7
can't fight the moon - light. Deep in the dark, you'll sur - ren - der your heart. Don't you know,
B
A
G♯
F♯m7
don't you know that you can't fight the moon - light, no, you can't fight
1.
2.
G♯7
G♯7
it. You can try it. It's gon-na get to your heart.

Blue

Words and Music by
Bill Mack

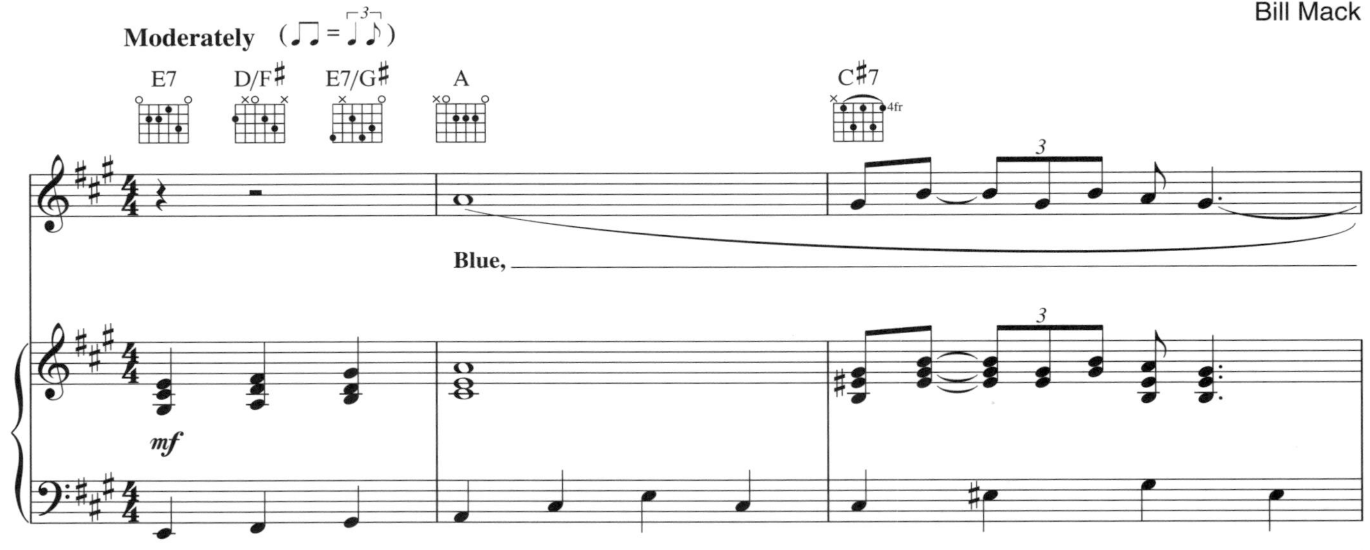

A
C#7
4fr
F#9
3fr
Blue,
oh, so
Instrumental solo
3
B7
E7
lone - some for you.
Tears fill my eyes
till I can't
A
D
A
N.C.
C#7
see.
Three o' clock in the morn
Now that it's o -
Solo ends
F#7
- ing
- ver,
here am I
I re - al - ized

B7
E7
To Coda
sit - ting here so lone - ly,
those weak words you whis - pered
so lone - some I could
were noth - ing but
D/F♯
E7/G♯
A
C♯7
4fr
cry.
Blue,
3
F♯9
3fr
B7
oh, so lone - some for you.
Why can't you be
D.S. al Coda
E7
A
E7
D7/F♯
E7/G♯
blue o - ver me?

CODA
F7
B♭
D7
lies.
Blue,
G9
C7
oh, so lone - some for you.
Why can't you be
F7
B♭
A
B♭
B
C7
blue o - ver me?
Why can't you be
F7
B♭
blue o - ver me?
rit.

Come Home Soon

Words and Music by
Kristyn Osborn and John Shanks

C D D C
E♭ F F E♭
tuck the kids in bed.
I don't know what you're do-
know that we're to-geth-
G D C G
B♭ F E♭ B♭
ing, and I don't know where you are.
er e-ven though we're far a-part.
But I look
And I'll wear
D C G C
F E♭ B♭ E♭
up at that great big sky and I hope you're wish-ing on that same
our luck-y pen-ny 'round my neck pressed to my heart.
D Am7 G/B Cadd9
F Cm7 B♭/D E♭add9
bright star.
I won-der,

Am7 G/B Cadd9 G
Cm7 B♭/D E♭add9 B♭
I pray. And I sleep a - lone, I cry
D/F♯ Em7 C
F/A Gm7 E♭
To Coda
a - lone.
1.2. And it's so hard liv - ing here on my own.
3. With - out you, this house is not a home.
So
G D/F♯ Em7 C
B♭ F/A Gm7 E♭
1.
please, come home soon, come home
2.
soon. I soon.

Em7 Cadd9 D G
Gm7 E♭add9 F B♭
I still i - mag - ine your touch.
D G D
F B♭ F
It's beau - ti - ful miss - ing some - thing that much.
But some - times love needs a fight -
Em C D
Gm E♭ F
D.S. al Coda
ing chance.
So I'll wait my turn un - til it's our turn to dance.
Coda
G D/F♯ Em7 C G
B♭ F/A Gm7 E♭ B♭
please.
(Come home...) I walk a - lone,
I

D/F#
Em7
G/C
F/A
Gm7
B♭/E♭
try a - lone,
and I'll wait
for you.
Don't want to die
a - lone.
G
D/F#
Em7
C
B♭
F/A
Gm7
E♭
So
please,
come home
G
D/F#
Em7
C
G
D/F#
B♭
F/A
Gm7
E♭
B♭
F/A
soon,
come home
soon,
(Please...)
Em7
C
G
Gm7
E♭
B♭
come
home
soon.
rit.

Does My Ring Burn Your Finger

Written by Buddy Miller
and Julie Miller

E5
D5
B5
not what you want - ed.
Now the
walls say your name, and the pic - tures are haunt -
ed.
Chorus:
1. 3. Does my ring burn your fin -
2. See additional lyrics
ger? Did my love weigh you down?
Was a

E5
D5
B5
F♯
prom - ise too much to keep a - round?
To Coda
B5
E5
D5
B5
1.
2.
2. I re -
E5
D5
B5

Bridge:
F♯
Please tell me, ba - by. Please tell me now. You say
E/G♯
E/B
E/D
E
D2
that I should just go on. Now, please tell me how.
B5
D.S. 𝄋 al Coda
3. Now it's just
Coda
B5
E5
D5

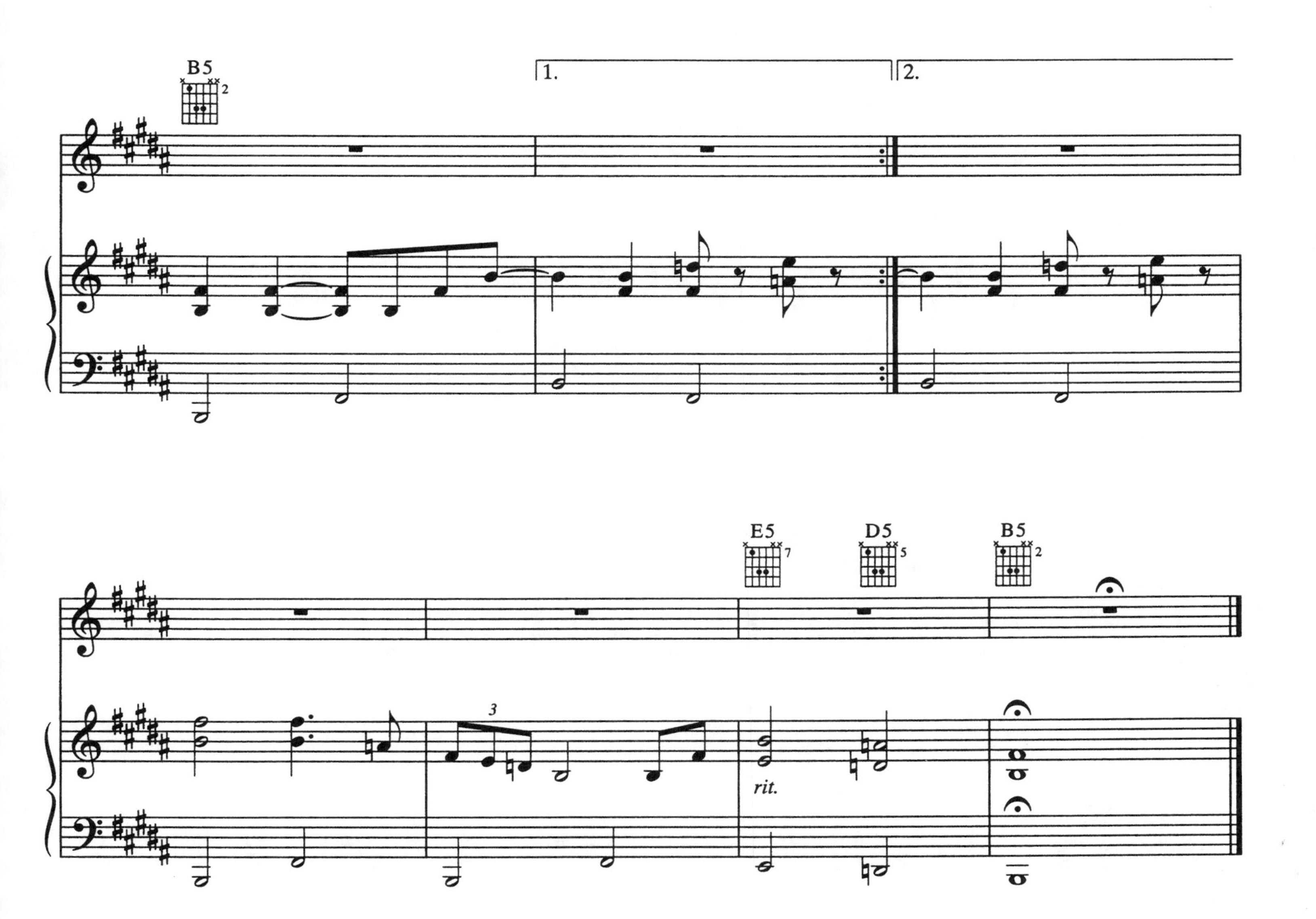

Verse 2:
I remember your words, and I can't keep from crying.
I could never believe that your kisses were lying.

Chorus 2:
Was there something from the past
Buried in a shallow grave?
Did you think that it was too far gone to save?
(To Bridge:)

Verse 3:
Now it's just me and the night, and I'm so broken hearted.
I just wait in the dark here for my dearly departed.
(To Chorus 3:)

Come On Over

Words and Music by
Shania Twain and R.J. Lange

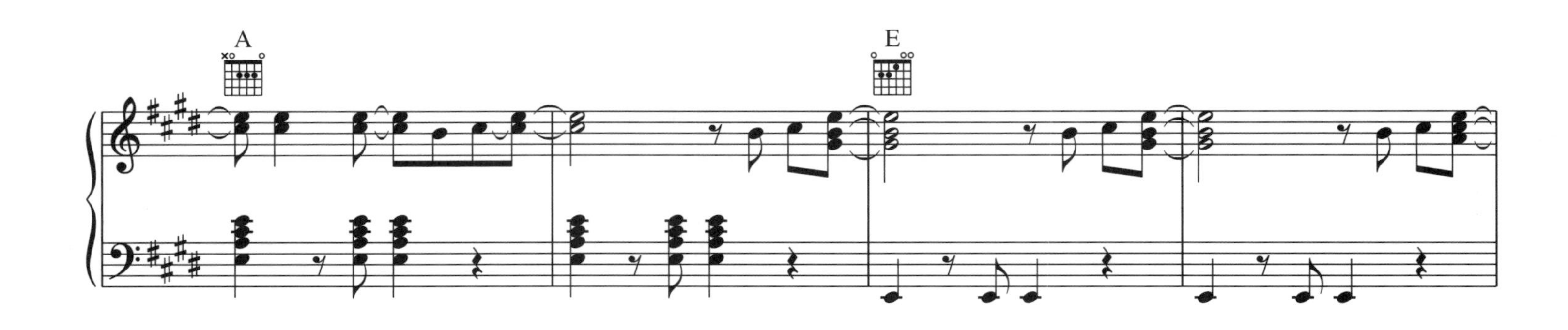

E
A
get a grip, get a - way some - where, take a trip.
E
Take a break, take con - trol, take ad - vice
A
E
from some - one you know. Come on o - ver,
A
come on in; pull up a seat, take a load off your feet.

E
A
Come on o - ver, come on in; you can un - wind, take a
F
load off your mind. Make a wish, make a move, make up
B♭
F
your mind, you can choose. When you're up, when you're down,
B♭
when you need a laugh, come a - round.

F
B♭
Come on o - ver, come on in; pull up a seat, take a
load off your feet. Come on o - ver, come on in;
you can un - wind, take a load off your mind. Oh,
oh.

F
B♭
Oh,
oh.
F♯
Be a win - ner, be a star, yeah, be hap -
get a grip, get a - way
B
- py to be who you are. Got - ta be
some - where, take a trip. Take a break,
F♯
your - self, got - ta make a plan, got - ta go
take con - trol, take ad - vice

B
F♯
for it while you can, yeah.
from some - one you know.
Come on o - ver,
come on in;
B
pull up a seat, take a load off your feet.
F♯
B
To Coda
Come on o - ver, come on in;
you can un - wind, take a
F♯
load off your mind.

B
F♯
B
D.S. al Coda
Get a life,
CODA
B
F♯
load off your mind, yeah.
Come on o-
B
-ver, come on in.
Yeah, come on, come on.

F♯
B
Oh,
oh.
N.C.
Oh,
B
F♯
oh.
Oh,
B
N.C.
oh,
come _ on
in.

He Rocks

Words and Music by
Troy Seals, Ted Hewitt
and Tracy Hagans

D
quite heav - en sent. Kind - a "Clark Kent." Yeah,
you 'cross the floor, charm you to the core,
G7
that's right.
for sure. Throw -
C
D
He's got the pro - file of an av - er - age Joe, but
in' on some make - up, kink - in' up my hair.
C
D
wick - ed on the week - ends when he's on a roll.
Come on, tax - i driv - er, you got - ta get me there.
He rocks!

G7
He kicks!
Born for a good time, and
D
G
he don't miss a lick. He can talk it, he can walk it, he can
G/B
C
throw down with the best. Gets you think - ing things that you
C♯°7
3fr
G
To Coda
nev - er will con - fess.
Send your ma - ma in - to shock.
Send your bod - y in - to shock.
Send your ma - ma in - to shock.

1.
D
G7
He rocks!
He rocks!
2.
G7
He's
C
D
D.S. al Coda
Oh,
he rocks!

Coda
D
G
C
(He rocks!)
Whoo.
G
D
Send your bod - y in - to shock.
He rocks!
G7
N.C.
3
G9
rit.

High on Love

Words and Music by
Kostas and Jeff Hanna

Original key: F♯ major. This edition has been transposed up one half-step to be more playable.

G
down.
And don't you know I'm high
on love
F
since you've come a-
C
round
D
and I ain't com-in' down.
G
C
D
Took a long time for me to be-lieve,

C
F/C
C
but I fin - 'lly got a re - prieve from lone - li - ness,
F/C
C
G
C
emp - ti - ness and wast - in' my time.
D
And I got luck - y one fine day.
Heav - en must have sent your love
my way and ev - er since, I've been rid - ing on

D
G
cloud nine.
High
on love
F
and I ain't com - in'
C
D
G
down,
no, I ain't com - in' down.
No, I ain't com - in' down,
C
D
no, I ain't com - in'

G
down.
High
on
love.
N.C.
C
G
D
C7
G

E♭
3 fr
C
G7
D
C7
G
C
D
It's the same old world turn-in'
round and a-round,
but my feet ain't touch-in' the ground.

Up in the sky without a care, just a couple of angels go - in' no - where.
G
High on love
N.C.
and I ain't com - in' down,
C
D
no, I ain't com - in'

G
down.
You keep on get - tin' me high
on love
F
since you've come a -
C
round
D
and I ain't com - in'
G
down.
No, I ain't com - in'
C
down,
D
no, I ain't com - in'

G
C
down, no, no, no. High
D
G
on love. No, I ain't com - in'
C
D
N.C.
G
down, no, I ain't com - in' down.

I Will...But

Words and Music by
Kristyn Osborn and Jason Deere

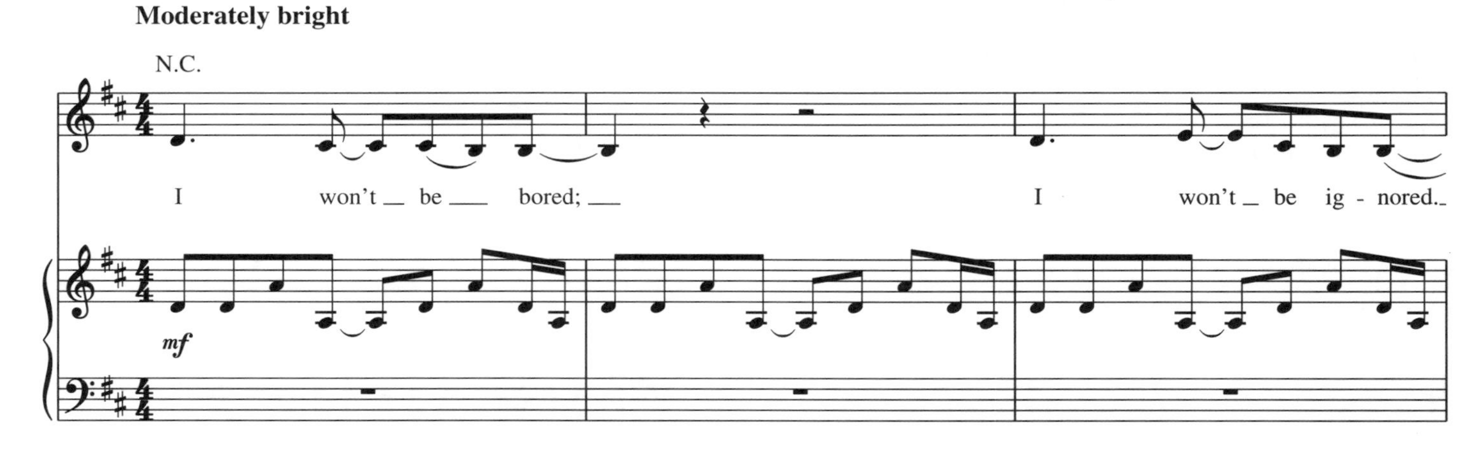

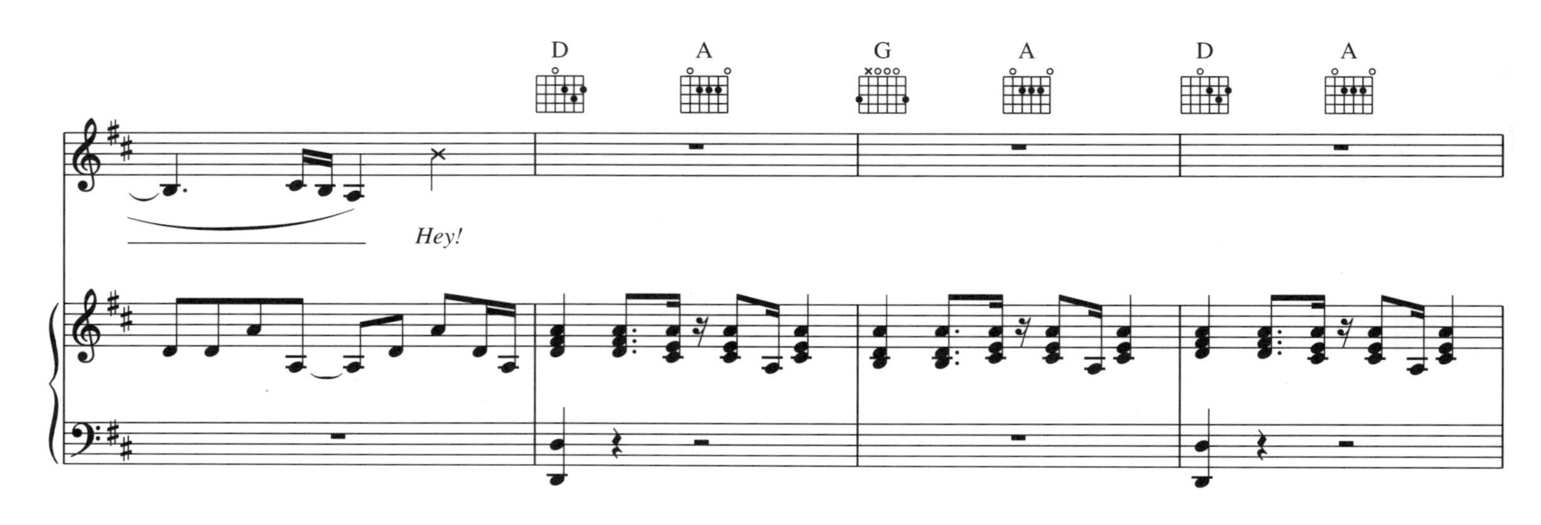

D A G A D A
I won't be your cure - all pill. And I won't run to fetch
I won't wear stil - let - to heels. I won't walk a mile
G A D A G A
the wa - ter just to tum - ble down the hill.
in your shoes just so I know how it feels.
D A G A D A
I won't be your Fri - day pay - check. I won't be the prize
I won't be your ob - li - ga - tion. I won't be your Bar -
G A D A G A
you flaunt. And I won't be your Mar - tha Stew - art, ba - by,
bie doll. I won't be the por - trait of per - fec -

D A G A
or your all - night res - tau - rant. But I will,
tion to a - dorn your wall.
D A G A D A
I will, I will be your ev - er - y - thing
(if you make me feel
G A D A G A
I will, I will, I will be the whole she - bang.
like a wom - an should.)
To Coda
1. 2.
Bm A G A G A
You know I will. But But

D
A
G
A
D
A
hey,
you know, you know I will,
all
G
A
D
A
G
A
D
A
right.
G
A
D
Tacet
I won't be your life - time girl - friend.
D
Tacet
I won't be just one of the guys.
D
Tacet
I won't be your ma -

G
D.S. al Coda
ma's fa - v'rite. I re - fuse to be the last in line. But I will,
Coda
G
A
D
A
G
A
Yeah, I will, I will, I will be your ev - er - y - thing.
D
A
G
A
D
A
I will, I will be the whole she - bang. I will, I will
G
A
D
A
G
A
be your ev - er - y - thing. I will, I will, I will, I

D A G A D A
will, yeah. You know I will, you
G A D A
know, you know I will. You know I will, you
G A D A G A
know, you know I will, yeah.
D A G A D

In My Daughter's Eyes

Words and Music by
James Slater

C D G C/G G G/B
D♭ E♭ A♭ D♭/A♭ A♭ A♭/C
strong and wise, and I know no fear. But the truth is
turns to light and the world is at peace. This mir - a - cle God
C D G D/F# Em7 G/D
D♭ E♭ A♭ E♭/G Fm7 A♭/E♭
plain to see, she was sent to res - cue me. I see who I
gave to me gives me strength when I am weak. I find rea - son
C D 1. G Cm6/G
D♭ E♭ A♭ D♭m6/A♭
wan - na be in my daugh - ter's eyes.
to be - lieve in my daugh - ter's
G Dsus4 G/B 2. G C/G G G/B
A♭ E♭sus4 A♭/C A♭ D♭/A♭ A♭ A♭/C
In my daugh - ter's eyes. And when she wraps her

Csus2
G/B
D♭sus2
A♭/C
hand a - round my fin - ger al - ways puts a smile in my heart. Ev - 'ry - thing be -
f
A9
A6
A7
C/D
B♭9
B♭6
B♭7
D♭/E♭
comes a lit - tle clear - er. I re - al - ize what life is all a - bout. It's hang - ing on when your
3
Cadd2
B
B/D♯
Em
D
D♭add2
C
C/E
Fm
E♭
heart has had e - nough. It's giv - ing more when you feel like giv - ing up. I've
C
D
Csus2
D♭
E♭
D♭sus2
seen the light. It's in my daugh - ter's eyes.
mf
mp

G/B
Em
G/D
C
D
A♭/C
Fm
A♭/E♭
D♭
E♭
G
Cm6/G
G
Cm6/G
A♭
D♭m6/A♭
A♭
D♭m6/A♭
mf
In my daugh - ter's
Cadd2
D
Gadd2
G
D♭add2
E♭
A♭add2
A♭
eyes I can see the fu - ture, a re -
C
D
G
C/G
G
G/B
D♭
E♭
A♭
D♭/A♭
A♭
A♭/C
flec - tion of who I am and what will be. And though she'll grow and

C
D
D/C
G/B
Em
G/D
D♭
E♭
E♭/D♭
A♭/C
Fm
A♭/E♭
some - day leave, may - be raise a fam - i - ly, when I'm gone I
C
D
B
B7/D♯
Em
Bm/D
D♭
E♭
C
C/E
Fm
Cm/E♭
hope you'll see how hap - py she made me, for I'll be
rit.
C
D
G
Cm6/G
D♭
E♭
A♭
D♭m6/A♭
there in my daugh - ter's eyes.
G
Cm6/G
G
A♭
D♭m6/A♭
A♭
rit.

Landslide

Words and Music by
Stevie Nicks

Eb
Bb/D
Cm7
Bb/D
3 fr
land - slide brought me down.
Oh,
Eb
Bb/D
Cm
Bb/D
mir-ror in the sky, what is love?
Can the child
Eb
Bb/D
Cm7
Bb/D
with-in my heart rise a - bove?
Can I
Eb
Bb/D
Cm7
Bb/D
sail through the chang - ing o - cean tides?
Can I

E♭
B♭/D
Cm7
B♭/D
3 fr
handle the sea - sons of my life?
Mm mm, I don't know.
Mm mm,
mm mm.
F7/A
Well, I've
B♭
Gm
been a - fraid of changing - ing 'cause I

Eb
Bb/D
Cm7
F7/A
3fr
built my life a-round you. But time
Bb
F7/A
Gm7
makes you bold - er. Chil - dren get old - er and I'm
Eb
Bb/D
Cm7
To Coda
Bb/D
get-ting old - er, too. So...
Ebsus2
Bb/D
F5/C
Bb/D

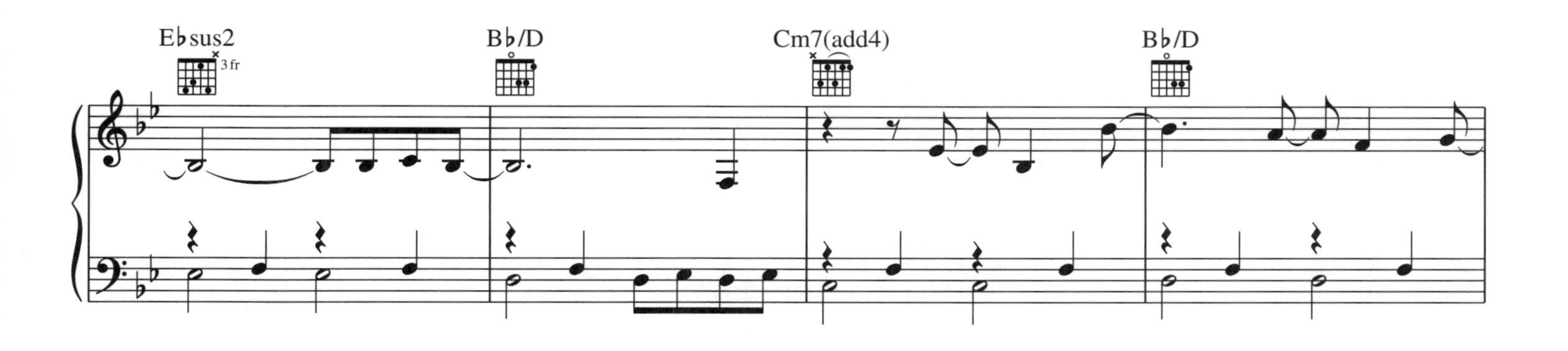
Eb sus2
3 fr
Bb/D
Cm7(add4)
Bb/D

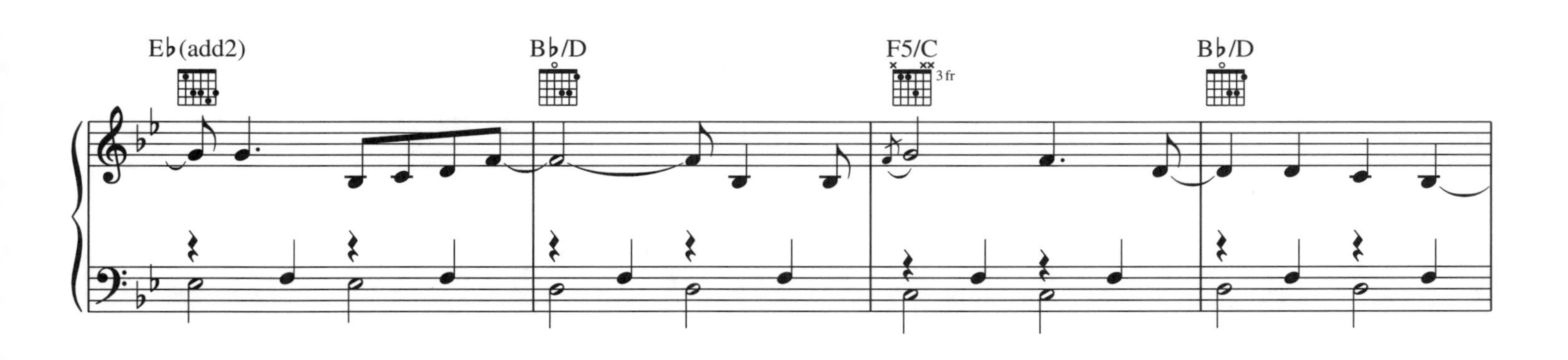
Eb(add2)
Bb/D
F5/C
3 fr
Bb/D

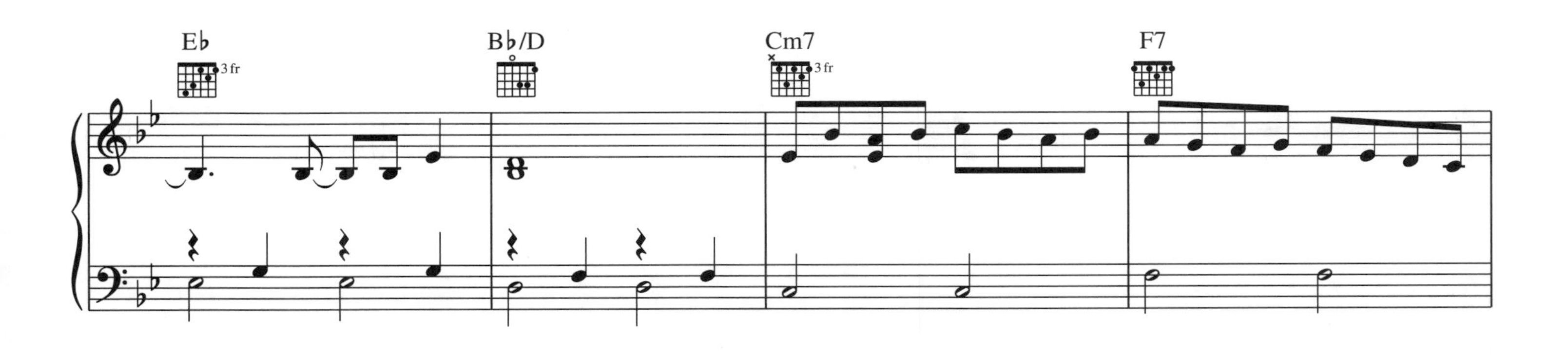
Eb
3 fr
Bb/D
Cm7
3 fr
F7

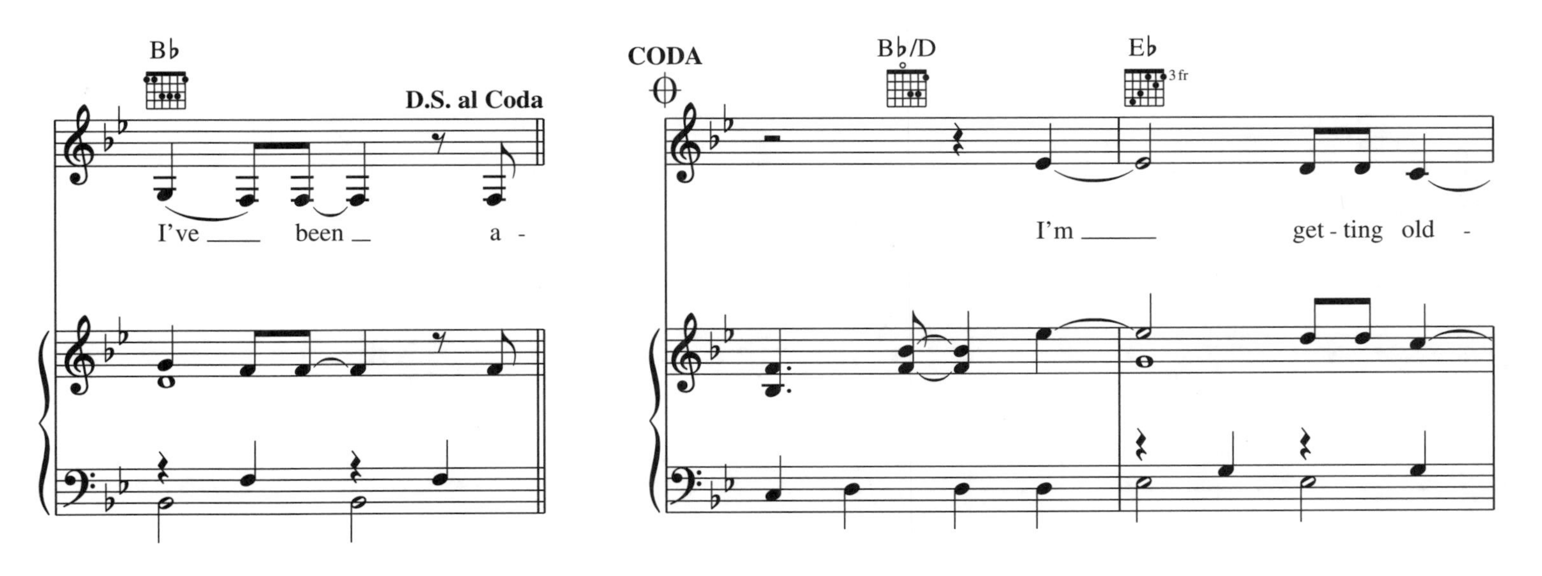
Bb
D.S. al Coda
I've been a -
CODA
Bb/D
Eb
3 fr
I'm get - ting old -

B♭/D
Cm7
B♭/D
E♭sus2
3 fr
- er, too. So take this love,
F5/C
Oh, if you climb a moun -
take it down.
Fsus/C
E♭
- tain and you turn a - round, if you see my re - flec -
- tion in the snow - cov - ered hills, well, the land - slide will

B♭/D
Cm7
B♭/D
E♭
3fr
bring it down, down. And if you see my re-flec-
B♭/D
Cm7
Freely
B♭/D
tion in the snow - cov-ered hills,
rall.
Tempo 1
E♭
B♭/D
Cm7
well, may-be the land - slide 'll bring it down. Well,
B♭/D
E♭
B♭/D
Cm
well, the land - slide 'll bring it down.
rall.

Let's Make Love

Words and Music by
Bill Luther, Aimee Mayo,
Chris Lindsey and Marv Green

Gm
Dm/F
E♭
The on - ly thing I wan - na do is
B♭/F
F
E♭
E♭6
be with you, as close to you as I can
E♭maj7
E♭
B♭
be. And let's make love all night
F
Gm
long un - til all our strength is gone.

E♭
3fr
B♭
And hold on tight, just let
F
Gm
3fr
go. I wan - na feel you in my soul.
E♭
3fr
Cm7
3fr
B♭/D
E♭
3fr
F
Un - til the sun comes up, let's make
B♭
F/A
Gm
3fr
B♭/F
love.
3

E♭6/9
F6
G
(Male:)
Do you know what you
D/F♯
Em
G/D
C
do to me?
Ev - 'ry - thing in - side of me
G
D/F♯
is want - ing you
and need - ing you.
Em
G/D
C
I'm so in love with you.

G/D
D
Look in my eyes, let's get lost to - night
C
C6
Cmaj7
C
G
in each oth - er. Both: Let's make love all night
D
Em
long un - til all our strength is gone.
C
G
Hold on tight, just let

D
Em
C
To Coda
(Male:)
go. I wan-na feel you in my soul. Un-
Am7
G/B
C
D
G
F/A
Both:
til the sun comes up, let's make love.
B♭
F/A
Gm
3fr
B♭/F
Dsus
N.C.
D.S. al Coda
Let's make

CODA
Am7
G/B
C
(Female:) Oh,
til the sun comes up, (Female:) un -
Am7
G/B
Csus2
Dsus
til the sun comes up, Both: let's make
G
D/F#
love.
3
Em
Csus2
G
(Male:) all night long,
(Female:) Let's make love all night long. Let's make love.
rit.

Little Good-byes

Words and Music by
Kristyn Osborn, Kenny Greenberg,
and Jason Deere

G
Cadd9
D
A♭
D♭add9
E♭
one last min - ute of my time in this mess I left be - hind.
Em7
A7
Fm7
B♭7
When you come home to - night and turn on the light,
Em7
D
Fm7
E♭
don't you be sur - prised to find my lit - tle good -
G
Cadd9
D
Cadd9
A♭
D♭add9
E♭
D♭add9
byes, my lit - tle good -
Emp - ty hang - ers by the clos - et door, lip - stick tube on the bath - room floor,

G
Cadd9
D
Ab
Dbadd9
Eb
byes,
oh, my
un - paid bills by the kitch-en phone.
I took the Beat-les, left Bil - ly Joel.
C
lit-tle good - byes,
lit-tle good-, lit-tle good - byes.
I'm sure you're sure I'll be back in just an hour or two.
You'll tape a
Db
Hall - mark to my door;
they al-ways said it bet - ter than you.

G
Cadd9
D
Cadd9
A♭
D♭add9
E♭
D♭add9
And if you're won - d'rin' when you're gon - na hear from me, well, take a
real good look a - round, boy, and it won't be hard to see.
Em7
A7
Fm7
B♭7
When you come home to - night and turn on the light,
don't you be sur - prised to find my lit - tle good -

G Cadd9 D Cadd9
A♭ D♭add9 E♭ D♭add9
byes, my lit - tle good -
Took your fa - v'rite Dodg - ers hat, left the lit - ter but I took the cat.
G Cadd9 D Cadd9
A♭ D♭add9 E♭ D♭add9
byes, yeah, my
Load-ed up the T - V in the back of my car. Have fun watch-in' the V - C - R.
G Cadd9 D Cadd9 G Cadd9
A♭ D♭add9 E♭ D♭add9 A♭ D♭add9
lit-tle good - byes, lit-tle good -, lit-tle good - byes.
D Em7
E♭ Fm7
So cry to your ma - ma and your

A7
B♭7
Em7
Fm7
sym - pa - thet - ic friends and tell 'em, tell 'em how the sto - ry
D
E♭
C
D♭
G
A♭
Cadd9
D♭add9
ends. My lit - tle good - byes,
Took the hour - glass, left the sand; now
my lit - tle good - byes,
you got time on your hands. Took the stat - ue from Ja - pan,
woh, my lit - tle good - byes.
fun - ny lit - tle Bud - dha man. Change my voice on the ma - chine or there'll be

D Cadd9 G Cadd9
E♭ D♭add9 A♭ D♭add9
lit - tle good - byes with ev - 'ry ring. Left the pic - tures and took the frames. I've
D G F Cadd9 D
E♭ A♭ G♭ D♭add9 E♭
got the um - brel - la; here comes the rain, yeah, yeah, yeah.
Lit - tle good -
G F Cadd9 D G F
A♭ G♭ D♭add9 E♭ A♭ G♭
byes, lit - tle good - byes.
Hey, hey, yeah, yeah, yeah. Hey, hey,
Cadd9 D G F Cadd9 D G
D♭add9 E♭ A♭ G♭ D♭add9 E♭ A♭
yeah, yeah, yeah. Hey, hey, yeah, yeah, yeah, lit - tle good - byes.

Man! I Feel Like A Woman!

Words and Music by
Shania Twain and R.J. Lange

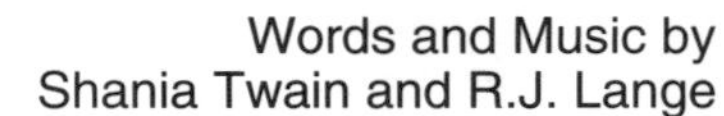

- ly raise my voice. Yeah, I wan - na scream and shout.
Eb5
Bb5
N.C.
Ah! No
Bb5
in - hi - bi - tions, make no con - di - tions. Get
need a break. To - night we're gon - na take the
Eb5
Bb5
a lit - tle out - ta line. I
chance to get out on the town. We

ain't gon - na act po - lit - i - c'lly cor - rect. I on -
don't need ro - mance, we on - ly wan - na dance. We're gon -
- ly wan - na have a good time.
na let our hair hang down.
Eb5
Bb5
Ab
4fr
The best thing a - bout be - ing a wom - an
Bb
in the pre - rog - a - tive to have a lit - tle fun and...

F
Oh, oh, oh, go to-tal-ly cra - zy,
for - get I'm a la - dy,
men's shirts, short
Dm
Bb
skirts. Oh, oh, oh, real-ly go wild, yeah, do - in' it in
F
style. Oh, oh, oh, get in the ac - tion,
feel the at-trac - tion.

Dm7
Col-or my hair, do what I dare. Oh, oh, oh, I wan-na be free, yeah, to
To Coda
Bb
Gm7
3fr
1
N.C.
Bb5
feel the way I feel. Man! I feel like a wom-an.
Eb5
The girls
2
N.C.
Ab5
4fr
Eb5
Man! I feel like a wom-an.
Instrumental solo

B♭5
A♭5
4 fr
E♭5
D.S. al Coda
Solo ends
CODA
Gm7
3 fr
feel.
(Do the way I feel.)
N.C.
Man! I feel like a wom - an.
B♭
A♭
1,2
E♭
3
I feel like a wom - an.

My Baby Thinks He's a Train

Written by Leroy Preston

Up tempo Country Rock

mf

It's

F

three A. M. in the morn - ing a
Choo choo ain't just some train sound. It's the

F6 F

train whis - tle is blow - in' It
noise that you hear when my ba - by hits town, With his

Bb
Bb7
sounds like some lone - some song I got in my
long hair fly - in' man he's hard to
F
C7
soul
tame
My ba - by split the blan - ket He
What you s'pose to do when
Bb7
F
won't be back no more
your ba - by thinks he's a train
F
My ba - by thinks he's a train
He eats mon - ey like a train eats coal
He
He

F6
makes a whis - tle stop then he's gone a - gain
burns it up and leaves you in the smoke. If you
Bb9
Some - times it's hard on this poor girls
want to catch a ride You wait 'til he un -
F
brain (this poor girls brain) I'm tell - ing you boys
winds But he's just like a train
Bb7
F
My ba - by thinks he's a train
He al - ways gives some bum a ride.

B♭
F
Lo - co - mo - tion is the way he moves He drags me a - round
F
F7
B♭
like an old ca - boose I'm tell - ing you girls that girl's in - sane
F
G7
My ba - by thinks he's a train
F
1
2

Simple Life

Words and Music by
Aimee Mayo, Hillary Lindsey,
Chris Lindsey and Troy Verges

G5
3fr
But there's noth - in' like com - in' home,
D5
5fr
D
N.C.
noth - in' like com - in' home.
I wan - na
D5
5fr
sit on my front porch and drink my lem - on - ade.
Cut my
blan - ket down to the creek
and let the
grass af - ter church ev - 'ry Sun - day.
And go out Sat - ur - day
wa - ter sing me to sleep
and let go of time.

G5
3fr
D5
5fr
night.
Live the sim - ple life.
Live the sim - ple life.
Bm
A/C♯
D
Wake up in the morn - in' to these
Well, late - ly I've seen too man - y
G
Bm
A/C♯
D
A
fields of gold and take a long walk down a grav - el road.
cit - y lights. I wan-na go some - where where I can see the stars at night.
D
Bm7
Spend my days in sweet sun - shine and rock in my swing and watch my gar - den grow.

A
Know that I'll al - ways have some - one to hold. Oh, I
G
1
D5
5fr
wan - na live a sim - ple life.
Da da da da da da da. I wan-na take a
2
D5
5fr
wan - na live a sim - ple life.

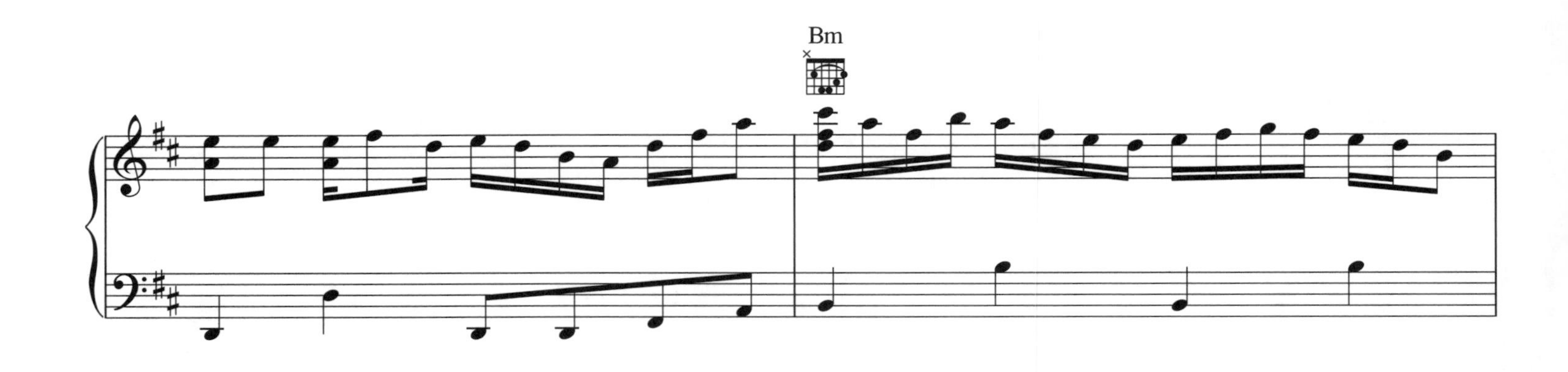
Bm

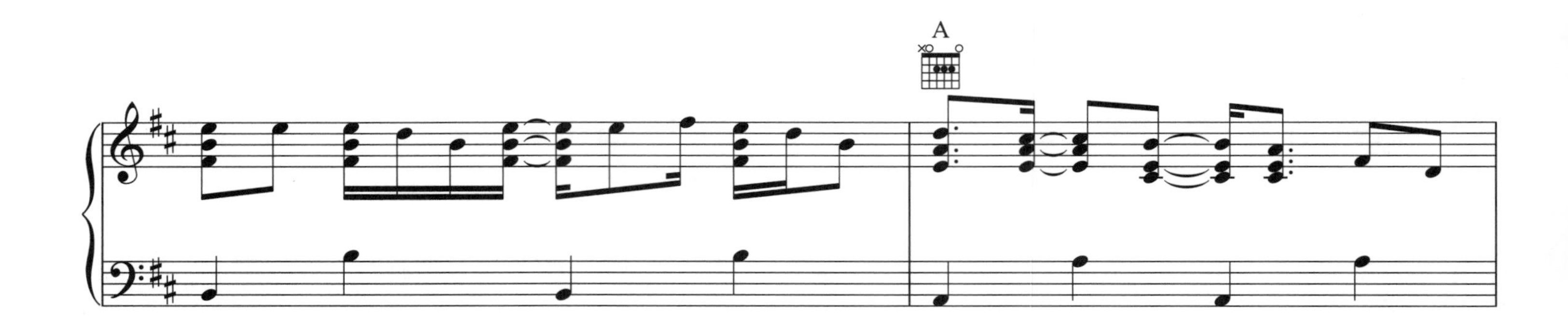
A

G

Bm7
Spend my days in the sweet sun -

D/A
shine, rock in my swing and watch_ my ba - bies grow.
G
Know that I'll al-ways have_ some, some - one to hold.
D
N.C.
D
3
Oh, spend my days in sweet sun - shine and rock
3
Bm7
in my swing and watch_ my gar - den grow.

A
G
Know that I'll al - ways have some - one to hold. Oh, I
wan - na live a sim - ple, I
D
wan-na live a sim-ple life.
Da da
D5
5fr
da da da da da da.

This One's for the Girls

Words and Music by
Aimee Mayo, Hillary Lindsey
and Chris Lindsey

A♭
D♭
E♭
High school can be so rough, can be so mean.
Fm
D♭
Hold on to, on to your in - no - cence.
E♭sus
E♭
E♭sus2
E♭
Fm
Stand your ground when ev -
D♭
E♭sus
E♭
- 'ry - bod - y's giv - in' in. This one's for the girls.

A♭
D♭
E♭
4fr
3fr
This is for all you girls a - bout twen - ty - five
This is for all you girls a - bout for - ty - two,
in lit - tle a - part - ments, just try -
toss - in' pen - nies in to the foun -
- in' to get by. Liv - in' on, on dreams
- tain of youth. Ev - 'ry laugh, laugh line
Fm
and Spa - ghet - ti - O's. Won - d'rin' where
on your face made you who
E♭sus
E♭sus2
6fr

Fm
Db
Ebsus
6fr
Eb
3fr
your life is gon - na go.
you are to - day.
This
one's for the girls
Ab
4fr
Ab/C
3fr
who've ev - er had a bro - ken heart,
Db
Fm
Eb
3fr
Ab
4fr
who've wished up - on a shoot - ing star.
You're beau -
Ab/C
3fr
Db
Eb
3fr
ti - ful the way you are.
This one's for the girls

A♭
A♭/C
4fr
3fr
who love with - out hold - in' back,
D♭
Fm
E♭
3fr
who dream with ev - 'ry - thing they have,
D♭
all a - round the world.
E♭sus2
E♭
6fr
3fr
To Coda
This one's for the girls.

1
A♭
4fr
D♭
(This one's for all the girls.)
E♭
3fr
2
D♭
Yeah,
A♭/C
3fr
E♭
3fr
we're all the same in - side (The same in - side.)
D♭
A♭/C
3fr
E♭5
6fr
E♭
3fr
from one to nine - ty - nine. This

D.S. al Coda
CODA
A♭
4fr
one's for the girls.
(This one's for
D♭
E♭
3fr
all the girls.)
Yeah, this one's for the girls.
A♭
4fr
D♭
(This one's for
all the girls.)
E♭
3fr
Fm
E♭
3fr
A♭
4fr

This Kiss

Words and Music by
Annie Roboff, Beth Nielsen Chapman
and Robin Lerner

A
F♯m7
E
E/G♯
straight a - cross the sky.
I'm for - ev - er yours.
It's the way you love me.
A
B
E
E/G♯
A
B
It's a feel-ing like this.
It's cen - trif - u - gal mo - tion.
It's per - pet - u - al bliss.
E
E/G♯
A
B
E
E/G♯
It's that piv - ot - al mo - ment.
It's ah,
im - pos - si - ble.
un - think - a - ble.
This kiss, this kiss,
A
C♯m
B
E
E/G♯
1
A
C♯m
B
4fr
un - stop - a - ble.
un - sink - a - ble.
This kiss, this kiss.

2
A
C♯m
4fr
B
C
Am7
D/F♯
G
You can kiss me in the moon-light, on the roof-top, un-der the sky, oh.
C
Am7
D/F♯
G
You can kiss me with the win-dows o-pen while the rain comes blow-in' in-side, oh.
C
C/B
Am7
G
D/F♯
G
Kiss me in sweet, slow mo-tion. Let's let ev-'ry-thing slide.
F♯m7
F♯m7/B
You got me floating, you got me fly-ing.

F# F#/A# B C# F# F#/A#
It's the way you love me. It's a feel-ing like this. It's cen-trif-u-gal mo-tion.
B C# F# F#/A# B C# F# F#/A#
It's per-pet-u-al bliss. It's that piv-ot-al mo-ment. It's, ah, sub-lim-i-nal. This kiss, this kiss.
B D#m C# F# F#/A# B D#m C# F# F#/A#
It's crim-i-nal. This kiss, this kiss. It's the way you love me,
Repeat and Fade
Optional Ending
B D#m C# F# F#/A# B D#m C# F#
ba - by. It's the way you love me, dar - ling.

This Woman Needs

Words and Music by
Kristyn Osborn, Bonnie Baker
and Connie Harrington

D/F#
Em
melts with your touch wants you to feel what I'm feel - ing right
in ev - 'ry light and hear that you still think I'm beau - ti - ful
C
G
now.
an - y - way.
'Cause this wom - an needs a safe place to
mf
Bm
C
Cm
3 fr
land, the strength in your hands to know you know. What
G
Bm
this wom - an needs is some - where to cry. So

C
Em
lay by my side and I'll tell you, I'll
1.
F
2.
F
tell you. This wom - an tell you what this wom - an
G
Bm
C
needs.
Cm
3 fr
G
Oh, what this wom - an needs is some - where to

Bm
C
cry. So lay by my side and I'll
Em
F
G
tell you, I'll tell you what this wom - an needs.
Cm
G
Yeah, what this wom - an needs.
Freely, slowly
Cm
N.C.
G
Yeah, yeah, yeah, what this wom - an needs.
mp

Wide Open Spaces

Words and Music by
Susan Gibson

F♯m7
E/G♯
Who's nev - er left home, who's nev - er struck out to find a
A
E
A
dream and a life of their own, a place in the clouds, a foun - da -
A/B
B
E
F♯m7
tion of stone?
Man - y pre - cede and man - y will
She trav - eled this road as a
E
F♯m7
fol - low,
child,
a young girl's dreams no long - er
wide - eyed and grin - ning, she nev - er
3

E
A
E
hol - low. It takes the shape of a place out west.
tired. But now she won't be com - ing back with the
A
But what it holds for her she has - n't yet
rest. If these are life's les - sons, she'll take this
A/B
B
E
F♯m7
guessed.
test.
She needs wide o - pen spac -
A
B
E
F♯m7
- es, room to make her big mis -

A
B
E
F♯m7
- takes. She needs new fac -
es. She knows the high stakes.
1
2
stakes. She knows the high stakes.

F♯m7
E
F♯m7
E
F♯m7
A/B
E
A/C♯
E
As her folks drive a - way, her dad yells, "Check the oil."
A/C♯
E
Mom stares out the win - dow and says, "I'm leav - in' my girl." She said, "It

A
E
A
did-n't seem like that long a - go"
when she stood there
and let her own
A/B
B
E
F♯m7
A
B
folks know she need - ed
wide o - pen spac - es,
E
F♯m7
A
B
room to make her big mis - takes.
She needs
E
F♯m7
A
B
new fac - es.
She knows the high

E
F♯m7
A
B
stakes. She knows the high stakes, she knows the high
E
F♯m7
A
B
E
F♯m7
stakes. Wide o - pen spac - es, she knows the high stakes,
A
B
E
F♯m7
A
B
she knows the high stakes, wide o - pen spac - es.
E
F♯m7
A
A/B
E